FERRARI

Lee Stacy

Rourke
Publishing LLC
Vero Beach, Florida 32964

LIBRARY OF CONGRESS CATALOGING-IN-PUBLICATION DATA
Stacy, Lee, 1961-
    Ferrari / Lee Stacy.
        p. cm. -- (Hot cars)
    Includes bibliographical references and index.
    ISBN 1-59515-210-5 (hardcover)
    1. Ferrari automobile--Juvenile literature. I. Title. II. Series.

TL215.F47S726 2004
629.222'1--dc22

                                                    2004013021

For The Brown Reference Group plc

Managing Editor: Tim Cooke
Design Manager: Lynne Ross
Children's Publisher: Anne O'Daly
Production Director: Alastair Gourlay
Editorial Director: Lindsey Lowe

Picture Credits:
IMP AB

Printed in the USA

Some words are shown in **bold**, like this. You

can find out what they mean by looking at the

bottom right of most right-hand pages. You

can also find most of the words in the Glossary

on page 30.

Contents

Introduction

The Italian car company Ferrari is one of the most famous names in motor sport. Enzo Ferrari (1898–1988) began his career as a race driver in the 1920s. In 1929 he started his own racing team, but soon he also started making cars. For Enzo, however, racing always came first. He used the money he made from Ferrari sports cars to pay for his Formula One (F1) racing team.

The logo was first used by World War I flying ace Francesco Baracca. He later gave it to Enzo Ferrari.

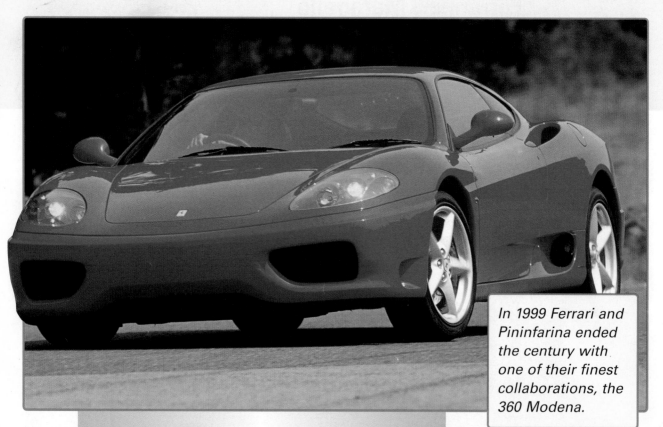

In 1999 Ferrari and Pininfarina ended the century with one of their finest collaborations, the 360 Modena.

Ferrari sports cars have become legendary, partly because of how they look. For over 30 years Ferrari has used the Italian-based design company Pininfarina to produce sleek cars. A Ferrari offers the road driver the fantasy of being a true racing champion. Some of the most famous models include the F355, 360 Modena, F50, Testarossa, 308, and 550 Maranello.

The F50 is one of the fastest sports cars ever made. Its top speed is 202 mph (325.1 km/h). It was built in 1997 to mark 50 years of Ferrari sports cars.

Ferrari's 308 was an important model. It used many technical improvements made in sports-car manufacturing from the mid-1970s to the mid-1980s.

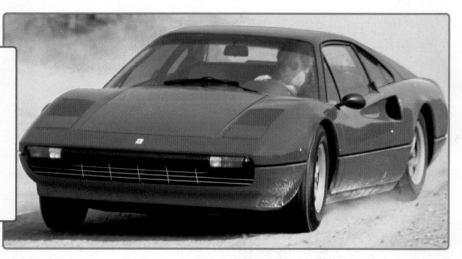

Ferrari F355

The F355 was introduced in 1994. It took the place of earlier models and was nearly as popular as the most famous Ferrari of all, the Testarossa. One reason car fans liked the new car was for its great power. The F355's V8 engine was smaller than the Testarossa's V12, for example, but mechanical and technical advances meant that it was more efficient. Head to head, the F355 could outrun the Testarossa with another 10 mph (16 km/h) to spare.

Milestones

Vital Statistics for the 1997 Ferrari F355 Spider	
Top speed:	183 mph (294.5 km/h)
0–60 mph:	4.7 seconds
Engine:	V8
Engine size:	213.3 ci (3,496 cc)
Power:	375 bhp at 8,250 rpm
Weight:	2,977 lb. (1,350 kg)
Fuel economy:	18.1 mpg

1965

The first of Ferrari's mid-range cars appears at the Paris Motor Show. Designed by Pininfarina, it is named for Enzo Ferrari's son, Dino.

1994

The F355 is introduced as Ferrari's latest mid-range model. The Dino had been replaced, in 1974, by the 308, which 11 years later was replaced by the 328. The F355 replaced the 1989 348.

1995

Ferrari unveils the F355 Spider, a convertible.

The sporty interior of the F355 has luxury leather seats and Ferrari's famous ball-topped stick shift.

Its performance is astounding but, unlike some supercars, the F355 is a usable size, has a gearshift that works easily, incredibly powerful brakes, and excellent handling.

In 1995 Ferrari added the Spider to the F355 range. The range already included the Berlinetta, which has a fixed top, and the GTS, which has a removable hardtop. The Spider is a **convertible** with a soft top that folds into an area behind the seats. Since its introduction, the Spider has become the most popular type of F355.

Convertible   A type of car that has a top that can be lowered or removed.

Specifications

The engineering of the F355 is impressive because of the power generated by Ferrari's 375-bhp, V8 engine. The outside of the car is equally impressive, thanks to the aerodynamic body designed by Pininfarina. The combination is fast and stylish.

Rear-mounted engine

The V8 engine in the F355 Spider is located behind the driver. This is the same for most Ferraris. One difference, however, is that the F355's engine is mounted lengthwise.

Small luggage area

The luggage space under the hood of the F355 Spider is small.

 The **suspension** system in the front and rear of the F355 is the shape of a double wishbone. It also has front and rear antiroll bars. Together the double-wishbone suspension and antiroll bars help to make the ride feel smooth.

The engine is made out of a lightweight metal called an alloy. It has 40 valves, five for each cylinder. The valves allow more fuel to the engine to give it maximum power.

Extra-wide wheels

At 18 inches (45.72 cm), the wheels are very wide, even for a sports car. The wheels are fitted with high-performance tires.

Stronger chassis

The **chassis** in the Spider is stronger than in the other F355s. It had to be stronger because the car does not have a hardtop, which makes the car body less strong and stable.

Downforce

Pininfarina designed the rear so that when the F355 is traveling at high speed, the air pushes down on the back of the car to keep it stable.

Chassis	The supporting frame of the car on which the body is fixed.
Suspension	A system of springs that support a car and make it travel more smoothly.

Ferrari 360 Modena

The last Ferrari introduced before the end of the 20th century was the 360 Modena. The car's name comes from a town in Italy. The engine is only a mid-sized V8, but it has a top speed of 185 mph (297.7 km/h) and can go from 0 to 60 mph (97 km/h) in 4.5 seconds. To achieve such efficient power, the engineers at Ferrari redesigned the engine for the 360 Modena. They also worked closely with the designers at Pininfarina, who gave the car a great **aerodynamic** shape.

Vital Statistics for the 1999 Ferrari 360 Modena

Top speed:	185 mph (297.7 km/h)
0–60 mph:	4.5 seconds
Engine:	V8
Engine size:	218.8 ci (3,586 cc)
Power:	394 bhp at 8,500 rpm
Weight:	3,065 lb. (1,390 kg)
Fuel economy:	16 mpg

Milestones

1967

The Dino 206 GT, the first Ferrari mid-engine model with a 2-liter V6 engine, proves very popular.

1973

Ferrari replaces the V6 engine with the more powerful V8, as used in the new 308 range.

1999

The latest V8 mid-engine model is the 360 Modena. It is the first Ferrari to have an all-aluminum construction. Compared to the F355, it is slightly larger but its new chassis means it is lighter.

The large paddles mounted on the steering column are used for shifting gears when the F1 gearbox is set on manual.

On the road the V8 comes on strong at 4,000 rpm, but doesn't run out of steam until 8,500 rpm. Combined with the in-street F1 gearshifts, the acceleration feels out of this world.

Pininfarina, the design company that has worked with Ferrari on several different models, has its own wind tunnel to test how air flows over differently shaped car bodies. By 1999 it had spent years getting the aerodynamics just right for the 360 Modena.

Aerodynamic   Designed to pass smoothly through the air.

Specifications

Ferrari created the 360 Modena to compete with the Porsche 911 Carrera. They were definitely successful. In head-to-head comparisons, the Ferrari outshines the Porsche. For example, at top speed the Ferrari is over 20 mph (32.2 km/h) faster than the German car.

V8 engine with 40 valves

The V8 engine has 40 valves, five in each cylinder. Three are used for taking in fuel and two for getting rid of **exhaust** fumes.

Luggage space

The luggage compartment in the 360 Modena is located under the hood.

To minimize the weight of the 360 Modena, aluminum was used in the suspension and the chassis.

The aerodynamics of the 360 Modena are impressive. According to wind-tunnel tests, the car has an extremely low drag coefficient of 0.34. Drag coefficient is a term used to describe how smoothly an object passes through the air.

Tested underside

Like the body of the car, the chassis of the 360 Modena was designed to be as aerodynamic as possible. To achieve this, Pininfarina spent many hours testing the underside of the car in a **wind tunnel**.

Fixed headlights

The headlights on the 360 Modena are fixed. Some earlier Ferraris had pop-up headlights, but testers discovered that pop-up lights created worse aerodynamics.

Exhaust   The gases created when an engine burns fuel; also used to describe the action of getting rid of the gases.

Wind tunnel   A testing area where air is blown at high speeds past an object.

13

Ferrari F50

Ferrari introduced the F50 in 1997 to celebrate 50 years of making some of the world's most sought-after sports cars. Although the new model was promoted as a street car, in reality it looked and performed more like a race car. With its powerful Formula 1 V12 engine, the F50 has a top speed of over 200 mph (321.9 km/h). Such a high performance is expensive. Ferrari only made a very limited number of F50s, and the cars sold for over $500,000 each.

Vital Statistics for the 1997 Ferrari F50

Top speed:	202 mph (325.1 km/h)
0–60 mph:	3.7 seconds
Engine:	V12
Engine size:	286.7 ci (4,698 cc)
Power:	513 bhp at 8,000 rpm
Weight:	3,080 lb. (1,397 kg)
Fuel economy:	12 mpg

The **cockpit** of the F50 is simple compared to most other Ferraris. Fewer gadgets and circuitry help lighten the weight of the car.

Milestones

1987

Ferrari introduces the F40 to mark the 40th anniversary of the company's first road car. At 200 mph (321.9 km/h), however, the F40 is more supercar than road car.

1990

Two years after Enzo Ferrari's death, the company begins looking at ways of turning the F1 V12 into a road car.

1997

To celebrate 50 years of making road cars, Ferrari brings out the limited-edition F50 with a modified F1 V12.

The F50, the supercar of supercars, is very user-friendly. The handling is not in the least twitchy but most of all you'll remember the incredible acceleration.

The F50 has a removable hardtop. Ferrari had to make sure that the F50's performance would not be any worse when the top is removed. To achieve this, they spent much time fine-tuning the car's design to improve its aerodynamics. The result is that, with or without its top, the F50 is one of the fastest cars on the road.

Cockpit   Area inside the car where the driver sits and operates the car.

Specifications

*The high performance of the F50 is due to a combination of technical advances. For instance, the engine is an improved V12, and the body is made out of lightweight carbon fiber. The car comes with a six-speed **transmission,** giving the driver total control.*

Adapted F1 brakes

The brakes are powerful disc brakes similar to those used until recently on F1 race cars. They have a rotating metal disc inside the wheel mechanism. The wheel is stopped by a device that pinches the disc.

Manual windows

Because the F50 is built for speed, the windows are manual, not electric. The unit that operates electric windows would have added extra weight to the car.

Rear wing

The large rear wing helps to press the car down on the road when traveling at high speeds.

Unlike most modern road cars, the Ferrari F50 does not have power steering.

The **radiator** is located in the front of the car, under the hood. Air is drawn in through the grille in the front of the car, then into the radiator. The used air leaves through the two large **vents** on the top of the hood.

Carbon-fiber body

Like F1 cars, the body of the F50 is made of carbon fiber. The material is lightweight but is stronger than steel.

Powerful V12 engine

A V12 engine mounted behind the driver gives real racing-car speed to the F50. the car can go from 0 to 60 mph (97 km/h) in 3.7 seconds and reach a top speed of 202 mph (325.1 km/h).

Radiator	A part of the engine-cooling system.
Transmission	The speed-changing gears that transmit power from the engine to the axle.
Vents	Openings that allow exhaust fumes to escape.

Ferrari Testarossa

From the mid-1980s until the mid-1990s the Testarossa was Ferrari's supercar. The engine was based on the V12 in Ferrari's **Formula 1** race cars, but it was modified for use on the road instead of the track. A couple of years before Ferrari ceased production of the Testarossa, the company came out with an improved and updated version. This Testarossa 512 M had greater engine performance and better brakes, but it still could not compete with Ferrari's new F50.

Milestones

1984

In collaboration with the car designers at Pininfarina, Ferrari creates the Testarossa. The model is shown at the Paris Motor Show.

1994

Ferrari introduces the F355, which outperforms the Testarossa. To compensate, the 512 M is brought out to breathe new life into the Testarossa range.

1996

The Testarossa range ends when Ferrari brings out the 550 Maranello.

Vital Statistics for the 1991 Ferrari Testarossa	
Top speed:	170 mph (273.6 km/h)
0–60 mph:	5.4 seconds
Engine:	Flat-12
Engine size:	301.6 ci (4,942 cc)
Power:	390 bhp at 6,300 rpm
Weight:	3,675 lb. (1,667 kg)
Fuel economy:	14 mpg

During the mid-1990s the Testarossa had one of the finest of all car interiors. It was described as a living room traveling at 170 mph (273.6 km/h).

No matter how fast you go, no matter what gear you're in, the Testarossa always seems to have more to come.

The 512 M, the last in the Testarossa series, was introduced in 1995 and was in production for only a couple of years. It had brakes that were much stronger than the previous models, so drivers could stop the car from a speed of 195 mph (313.8 km/h).

Formula One   A type of motor racing in which powerful, specially built cars race around circuits with many straights and corners, unlike the oval track used in Indy Car racing. Formula 1 races are known as Grand Prix. The American Grand Prix takes place each year.

Specifications

In its day, the Testarossa produced outstanding power for a road car. It was able to sprint from 0 to 60 mph in 5.4 seconds and to reach a top speed of 170 mph (273.6 km/h). The striking, aerodynamic body was the work of Pininfarina.

Front-mounted battery

The **battery** in the Testarossa is located in the front of the car, away from the rear-mounted engine. The arrangement distributes the weight of the car more evenly.

Pop-up headlights

The headlights pop up when they are turned on. This feature was dropped from some more recent Ferrari sports cars.

The wheels on the Testarossa are made of **alloy** and measure 16 inches (40.64 cm) in diameter. Also the rear tires are wider than the front ones.

The Testarossa was the widest high-speed sports car of its day. From 1984 to 1996, when it was in production, the car was 77.8 inches (197.6 cm) wide.

Slatted lights

The rear lights are slatted to match the side strakes. The strakes cover the vents on the sides of the car. The vents suck the air into the radiator.

Protective air-conditioning

Because the front windshield is so large, there is a risk that the cockpit could become overheated on hot sunny days. To prevent this, air-conditioning is a standard feature in the Testarossa.

Accessible engine

To help access the engine, the subframe, which supports the engine, is easily removable.

Alloy	A strong but lightweight metal made by mixing other metals.
Battery	The part of the engine that provides electrical power to start the car and to run its lights and other features.

Ferrari 308

The 308 replaced Ferrari's Dino in the mid-1970s. For a decade it was one of the company's most popular mid-range cars. Part of the 308's success was due to the car's design and technology from champion race-car driver Niki Lauda. Lauda's experience helped make the 308 special. Before production of the car ended in the mid-1980s, it went through several more improvements. For example, the engine grew from a V6 to a V8.

Vital Statistics for the 1977 Ferrari 308 GTS	
Top speed:	145 mph (233.4 km/h)
0–60 m.p.h:	7.3 seconds
Engine:	V8
Engine size:	178.6 ci (2,927 cc)
Power:	205 bhp at 7,000 rpm
Weight:	3,305 lb. (1,499 kg)
Fuel economy:	16.8 mpg

Milestones

1974
Ferrari begin collaborating with Pininfarina to create the 308 to replace the Dino.

1975
The 308 first appears at the Paris Motor Show.

1982
Because of environmentally friendly changes to the old 308, the car runs slower. To compensate, the engine in the new 308 is modified.

1985
Ferrari ends the 308 in order to make way for the 328.

The 308's interior was very basic and had room only for the driver and one passenger. The real interest lay in the 308's engine.

The performance of the Ferrari 308 is just what you want. With the high-revving V8 screaming toward its limit, 0 to 60 mph takes just over six seconds.

Ferrari used the body of the 308 for a racing car called the 288 **GTO**. The GTO was designed to run in a new class of race known as Group B. The Group B circuit never caught on with race fans, however, so the car did not get a chance to prove itself.

GTO   "Gran Turismo Omologato" is a term that was first used by Ferrari. It originally referred to cars that were meant for racing and that were not allowed to be driven on the road.

Specifications

The 308 was an important car for Ferrari. During the decade or so it was in production, there were many changes in sports-car design. Ferrari tried out several engine and mechanical innovations on the 308, such as the **fuel-injection** system.

Targa top

This version of the 308 has a Targa top. Targa tops are hardtops that can be removed. There is enough room to store the top under the hood.

Radiator placement

The radiator is located in the front of the car, under the hood. There is more room for it there than in the cramped engine compartment behind the driver. At the front, more air circulates around the radiator to help keep it cool.

Metal disc brakes

Both the front and rear wheels have vented metal disc brakes. Because the weight of the car is evenly distributed, the front brakes are the same size as the rear ones.

In 1981 the **carburetors** were replaced with a fuel-injection system. Fuel injection causes less pollution.

Air vents are on the the sides of the car behind the cockpit. The vent on one side of the car draws in air to help cool the engine. The other vent takes in air to cool the oil.

Pop-up headlights

When the 308 replaced the Ferrari Dino, one of the most noticeable differences between the two cars was the introduction of pop-up headlights. When down, the headlights give the front—or nose—of the car a flatter look.

Carburetor	A tube that mixes gasoline and air in the right proportions to make the combustible fuel for an engine. Modern cars no longer use carburetors.
Fuel injection	An electronically controlled valve that sends the right mix of air and fuel into the engine. It replaced the carburetor.

Ferrari 550 Maranello

Ferrari chose the name of the company's hometown, Maranello in Italy, for its first front-engined two-seater sports car since 1968. The 550 Maranello has a powerful V12 engine. The body was designed by Ferrari's longtime Italian-based collaborator, Pininfarina. After the F50, it is Ferrari's fastest car on the road.

Vital Statistics for the 1998 Ferrari 550 Maranello	
Top speed:	199 mph (320.3 km/h)
0–60 mph:	4.4 seconds
Engine:	V12
Engine size:	334 ci (5,474 cc)
Power:	485 bhp at 7,000 rpm
Weight:	3,726 lb. (1,690 kg)
Fuel economy:	11.8 mpg

Milestones

1996

The Testarossa comes to an end and is replaced by the 550 Maranello. To celebrate its launch, Ferrari hires a young German racing driver to show off the car at the company's Fiorano test track. Both the car and the driver, Michael Schumacher, impress critics.

1997

To meet a growing demand from wealthy clients for customized versions of the 550 Maranello, Ferrari offers a long list of luxury and performance options.

Easy-to-read dials, a stylish steering wheel, and fine leather seats are a few features that make the 550's interior impressive.

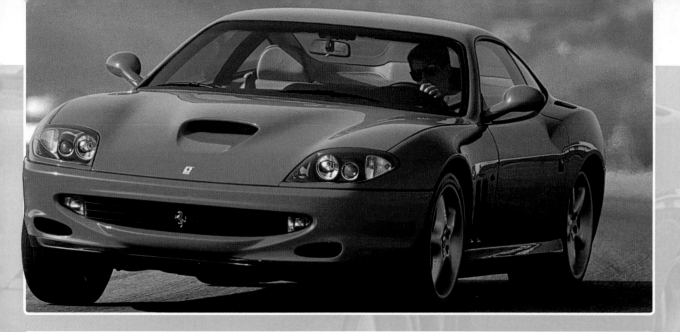

As well as blistering performance and a magnificently responsive V12 engine, the Maranello has a sensational chassis that is fluid and minutely adjustable at the throttle.

In the late 1990s the 550 Maranello, with its V12 engine, was the fastest Ferrari ever made. It could go from 0 to 60 mph in 4.4 seconds and its top speed was 199 mph (320.3 km/h).

Throttle   Another name for the accelerator.

Specifications

Pininfarina came up with an extremely aerodynamic design for the body of the 550 Maranello. However, the car's body is the one thing about the 550 Maranello that has divided critics. Some say it lacks Pininfarina's typical styling innovations.

Luxury cockpit

The interior is very comfortable and sophisticated. Leather upholstery, Sony multi-CD player, and electronically adjustable seats are just a few of the standard features.

Front-mounted engine

The 550 Maranello has an all-alloy V12 engine. It is mounted in the front of the car.

Unique wheels

Pininfarina came up with a unique design for the 550 Maranello's five-spoked wheels. The tires were also made especially for the car.

Pininfarina was asked by Ferrari to design a car that honored its Daytona model of the 1970s. The result was the 550 Maranello, with a six-speed manual transmission.

The body, which is aluminum, is welded to a steel frame. A special material called Feran was used in the welding. Feran was needed because aluminum cannot be welded using traditional methods.

Traction control

The rear wheels on the 550 Maranello have an automatic **traction** control. This stops the wheels from overspinning during acceleration.

Spacious trunk

Unlike most Ferraris, the 550 Maranello has a large trunk, with 6.5 cubic feet (0.184 cubic meters) of room for luggage.

Traction   The grip between a tire and the surface of the road.

29

Glossary

aerodynamic (AIR o dy NAM ik): *Designed to pass smoothly through the air.*

battery (BAT uh ree): *The part of the engine that provides electrical power. The electricity is used to start the car and to run the car's lights as well as other features.*

carburetor (KAR buh RAYT ur): *A tube that mixes gasoline and air in the right proportions to make the fuel for an engine. Modern cars no longer use carburetors.*

chassis (CHASS ee): *The supporting frame of the car on which the body is fixed.*

convertible (kun VERT uh bul): *A type of car that has a top that can be lowered or removed.*

exhaust (ig ZOST): *Gases created when an engine burns fuel; also used to describe the action of getting rid of the gases.*

fuel injection (FYU ul in JEK shun): *Electronically controlled valve that sends the right mix of air and fuel into the engine. It replaced the carburetor.*

GTO (JEE TEE OH): *"Gran Turismo Omologato," a term first used by Ferrari. It referred to cars that were meant for racing,* and that could not be driven on the road.

radiator (RAYD ee AYT ur): *Part of the engine-cooling system.*

suspension (sus PEN shun): *A system of springs that support a car and make it travel more smoothly.*

throttle (THROT ul): *Another name for accelerator.*

transmission (trans MISH un): *Speed-changing gears that transmit power from the engine to the axle.*

Further Information

websites

www.ferrari.com
Ferrari

www.ferrariclubofamerica.org
Ferrari Club of America

http://home.clara.net/nigelk/history.htm
History of Ferrari in Formula One

http://auto.howstuffworks.com/engine.htm
How Stuff Works: Car Engines

books

● Beck, Paul. **Uncover a Race Car: An Uncover It Book.** Silver Dolphin Books, 2003.

● Goodfellow, Winston. **Italian Sports Cars.** Motorbooks International, 2002.

● Henry, Alan. **Fifty Years of Ferrari: A Grand Prix and Sports Car Racing History.** Motorbooks International, 1998.

● Hicks, Roger, and Keith Bluemel. **The Complete Ferrari.** Motorbooks International, 2002.

Index